A Narrative from an Old Confederate

A Narrative from an Old Confederate

Memoirs of a Civil War Soldier from the Alabama 35th Infantry

James W. Harmon

Cedar Lake Classics

Copyright © 2023 by Cedar Lake Classics

This is a proofread and newly designed edition of a public domain work.

CONTENTS

ABOUT THIS BOOK   vii
FORWARD   ix

1 | Why They Fought   1

2 | Florence Mobilizes   3

3 | News from Virginia   6

4 | The 35th Alabama Organizes   8

5 | On to Corinth   11

6 | Grand Junction, Tennessee   14

7 | The Battle of Corinth   16

8 | In Camp Near Holly Springs   20

9 | March to Grenada   23

10 | Letter from Home   26

11 | Thinking from Home   28

12 | March to North Alabama   30

CONTENTS

13 | Capturing the White Horse Cavalry   33

14 | A Visit to Florence   35

15 | Hood's Tennessee Offensive   38

EPILOGUE   43
NOTES   45

ABOUT THIS BOOK

In 1915, Gustavus W. Dyer, an eccentric Vanderbilt University professor of sociology and economics and director of the Tennessee Department of Archives and History, developed a crude questionnaire and submitted it to surviving Civil War veterans. Seven years later John Trotwood Moore, who succeeded Dyer as director of the Tennessee archives and library in Nashville, began collecting a majority of the responses to the questionnaires which he hoped would lead to a "true history of the Old South." In the end, 1,648 individuals responded to Dyer and Moore's unique attempt to preserve the memories of the Civil War generation.[1] Among the respondents was Dr. James W. Harmon, a 79-year-old dentist from Lawrenceburg, Tennessee, who on April 22, 1922, submitted not only the completed questionnaire but also a 71-page, handwritten autobiographical account which he entitled "A Narrative from an Old Confederate."

Describing himself as "a broken down Old Man" and a father of three grown children, who "are all doing well and whom I'm not ashamed," Harmon had outlived most of his former comrades from the dreadful years of 1861 to 1865. Born in Maury County, Tennessee, in September 1843, James was the eldest of three children of Albert and Sarah (Turner) Harmon. His paternal grandfather, Daniel Harmon, a veteran of the War of 1812, moved his family from Petersburg, Virginia, to Florence, Alabama, where he established a carriage and buggy manufacturing business. Albert Harmon worked for his father as a furniture maker until the early 1850s, when he became disabled "in mind and body."[2] While living with his grandparents and parents in a frame, six-room house, located at the intersection of Locust and Tennessee Street,

ABOUT THIS BOOK

James attended local schools until the fall of 1860, when he enrolled as a cadet at LaGrange Military Academy. At the end of his first year which ended on July 4, 1861, James Harmon ranked fifth in his class.[3] But, as Harmon relates below, his time at LaGrange ended abruptly.

In transcribing Dr. J. W. Harmon's reminiscence a genuine effort has been made to remain faithful to the original 1922 text. Harmon's orthography, punctuation, and capitalization have been reproduced without alteration, and brief information about individuals and events mentioned by Harmon has been provided.

FORWARD

The years that have passed seem but a short while since the horrors of war were raging over our country. No pen can picture correctly the desolation that followed, nor tongue fully describe the terrors, the miseries, the heartaches and desolation that was brought about as its consequence. Many whom we knew to love, many who were our cherished companions have passed into eternity. The old folks are all gone, the young that have been left are now far advancing on the shady side of life, and in a short while must pass away and their children fill their places, who from legends and historical accounts can speak of the trials and hardships of their ancestors.

James W. Harmon

1

Why They Fought

The incidents here related are from personal experience, many being called to memory only from notes taken as well as from letters that were written during these trying times. When war was declared it became the duty of the youth and manhood of the country to enlist in the army.

I was a Tennessean by birth, but Alabama was my adopted state, and when the summons came I felt it a duty to obey, and contribute my humble efforts in serving the cause which every true Southerner held as just and sacred. An all-wise Providence saw fit that things should be changed from what was so earnestly desired, and we have bowed with reverence to His will.

We can but think of the terrible ordeals through which we passed; of the hardships endured, of the dangers faced; of the time that was lost, of prospects that were blighted; of the friends we have lost, and of our homes that were made desolate; yet 'tis a consolation to know that we were conscientious in our undertakings, believing we were doing right and were leaning on the arms of Patriotism to help our land, our cherished homes, and our Southern country; the land of our birth under whose arms we were protected, and on whose breast we were fostered and under such circumstances we could but take her chances and her destinies as our own.

No doubt should exist, but that our enemies at that time held as conscientious views as we did, and the principles they believed, were as sacred to them, as ours were to us, for had we been reared in the North, no doubt, many of us would have had the same opinions as they; and would have taken the same course; however, Dixie was our home, and whatever was thought to be her interest, we claimed it ours, therefore our fates were cast with the South.

2

Florence Mobilizes

The years 1860 and 1861 were all ablaze with excitement. Political parties were using every effort to carry out the plans that each thought was for the common good. Divisions and contentions sprang up. War clouds arose in the distant horizon, while days and months rolled on they became nearer and larger, with more threatening attitude, until at last in the spring of 1861, the fearful lightnings of war leaped forth over the land, and the clash of arms were the inevitable result.

Well do I remember the intense excitement of the year during the spring and summer, and the calls for volunteers, the raising of companies, and organizing of regiments which were hurried off to the seat of war. Many of our men and youth went there with bright anticipations looking on it lightly, thinking that in a short while they would return home, but many never saw their friends again. I was then a school boy, with an earnest desire for an education but it was not long before my school had to close and the prospects for an educations ruined, as the unholy war was spread gradually over the whole country. On April 29, 1861 I received these lines from my Mother, Mrs. Sarah Harmon–

Dear Son.

This is a beautiful morning and I have concluded to write you a few lines so that you may learn the news, also how we are getting along on this side of the Tennessee. There is much excitement here today. The streets are full of men, many of them going to the telegraph office and to the post office to learn what they can in regard to the war. The Presbyterian church bell will soon ring to call us to hear an address from Dr. Rivers[4] to the Lauderdale volunteers,[5] and after the address each soldier will be presented with a bible. They will leave at 2 O'clock this evening for Richmond Va. It is certainly a very solemn time among the people, and a deep interest is being felt. The college here will soon break up, for the boys are determined to go off to the war, and some of the Professors will go with them. Their Company is named the "University Grays."[6]

I was then made the possessor of the following letter from Miss Alice Harmon[7]

Florence Ala. June 16th 1861–

Dear Brother.

I received your letter and we were all glad to hear from you. Florence has been in a great deal of excitement lately. The streets have been full of people, and about two hundred volunteers on parade. Captain Houston[8] and his company left today on the two O'clock train for Richmond Va. and the other one, Captain O'Neil's,[9] left yesterday for the same place. May God bless and protect them.

On June 18th. 1861, the following extract from a letter came to hand from Maury County Tenn.

Dear Friend.

It is with great pleasure that I can inform you that good old Tennessee is doing her part most nobly and faithfully towards our glorious Southern Confederacy. I well knew that her gallant sons would not be anyways backward in defending her rights for which she is so much distinguished, being one of the earnest champions of our dear Sunny South.

3

News from Virginia

Military enthusiasm had at this time taken hold of the people, and great interest was manifested all over the country as to what would be best for the common good. It was not hard to see that all were emerging into a sea of uncertainty as to what would, or could be done. The clash of arms were at hand, and the continued war news, with the reports that could be heard, led us to believe that there was a good chance for school days to be ended at no distant day. Hopes for peace, and averting war had been blasted, yet we persevered trying to improve, and at the same time were anxiously awaiting the news that must come from Virginia, which then was the seat of war. Sad news soon comes, we learn of the death and wounding of a number of old friends and acquaintances. A home letter, from my Sister, Miss Alice Harmon, explains itself.

July 24, 1861–

Dear Brother:

I will tell you of the battle at Manassas Junction, one of the hardest that was ever fought in this country. A great many were killed and wounded on each side. One of the Companies that left here (Capt McFarland's) had ten killed and twenty three wounded.[10] I am told our army captured 5000 prisoners, and also took 1200 horses, 500 wagons, and provisions enough to feed 50000 men for a good while. Our men charged their batteries, captured their cannon and turned them on the enemy. They were completely routed, and were pursued by 1500 of our cavalry, running them for eight miles, and strewing them on the way. I am told we took 64 cannon and 25000 small arms. The fight lasted until 10 O'clock at night.

A young man belonging to McFarland's company, about 17 years of age, was taken prisoner by one of the enemy's officers. The officer ordered him to get up behind him, as he was horse back, and with a view of carrying his prisoner into the Federal lines. He mounted behind the man, and had gone but a short distance when he grasped the officer's pistol, then ordered him off the horse or he would kill him. The officer obeyed and then was taken– he and his horse– to Gen Beauregard. The horse was a fine animal, and Gen Beauregard now has that horse to ride in the place of one that was shot from under him. That was well done, was it not?

John Simpson and William Andrews[11] were among the killed in Captain McFarland's Company. Among the wounded were James Jackson, Wat Foster and Charles Stewart[12] Captain Huston's and Captain O'Neal's Companies had done some hard service the day before, therefore Gen. Johnston[13] did not put them in the fight that day.

4

The 35th Alabama Organizes

We had now begun to be convinced that a terrible war was on hand and no one could give an idea as to what the result would be. Both sides were making big efforts to prosecute it to the fullest extent. Powerful armies were coming to oppose the southern forces, and soon their advancing columns were approaching our homes. Fort Donalson fell, and the gallant Southern army of General Albert Sidney Johnston had taken its stand near Corinth Miss, while the enemy was massing forces in opposition to him, near Pittsburg landing on the Tennessee river. Our school could stand no longer, for the south called each one to arms, and soon the boys were organizing in a company at Lagrange our school headquarters, where they expected to be joined by a number of other companies, recently organized to form a regiment.[14] It was then the memorable battle of Shiloh was fought, something over fifty miles from where our regiment was organizing and drilling, so as to be prepared for early duty in our army. It seems but yesterday when the awful peals of cannonading could be heard, so distinctly, that came from that awful field of death. For two long days it appeared as if the heavens were constantly muttering their thunder tones, and well it was known that many a gallant soldier was offering his life there. The time had then come for us to give a helping hand in the great struggle that was going on. Our company was composed mostly of young men and youths from leading and well to do families of North Alabama, and was formed at LaGrange, which was situated on a spur of the Cumberland mountains, being the place where many of us had so earnestly labored with studies during the past year, and also was the place selected as a camp of instruction. Our regiment also was organized at this place and then joined the army at Corinth.[15] Having visited my homefolks at Florence for a short while, I then started off to go with my company. Leaving home, I proceeded to Tuscumbia, which place was found to be full of stir and excitement. After reaching LaGrange I wrote my Mother the following letter.

LaGrange, Ala. March 23d. 1862.

My Dear Mother–

Having a chance to send a letter, it is with pleasure I write to inform you of my safe arrival here. Rather a bad time was experienced on the trip, however I got along safely. After leaving Florence the trip was made without hindrance, until we reached the suburbs of Tuscumbia. There we found the Rail Roads completely covered with trains. My friend and I walked to the Franklin house, and there the streets were found to be full of soldiers and the Rail Roads still blocked with trains. A great many soldier tents had been erected about the place. I looked around to see if any train was going up the road, and was told a freight train would soon be off in the direction we wished to go. It was noticed also that one company was getting on that train, so both of us, after placing our baggage on a coal car and then getting on it, we sat there for an hour or such a matter, expecting every minute to start. At last the train commenced moving, but it was only for a short distance for the purpose of unloading some freight.

We staid in the cold waiting for them to unload for an hour or so, and by that time they had unloaded, but they went back then to the same place from where they had first started. The Engineer then told us he did not know when he would be able to leave. After staying in the cold wind until Eight O'clock at night, we entered an old box car that had some straw in it, but found it very uncomfortable. Staying there about two hours, which was about ten O'clock, we concluded to leave, and then went to the hotel, but dared not leave the rail road, for there were sentinels posted all around. Having sat in the Franklin house until about 2. O'clock that night, then a passenger train came along and we boarded it, but found it so crowded, there was scarcely standing room. Arriving at Leighton I came within an ace of being left on the train, for the cars hardly stopped a minute, and not more than one half the men got off, the bell was rang and the train stopped again for a few seconds, and then started before I was able to get off, but I jumped off however, and walked here by day light, although the walk was quite muddy and disagreeable.

5

On to Corinth

Some of us had now realized our first experiences of hardships connected with a soldier life. The beginning had come, and our part then was to face it, and bear it like men. In a short while many were drilling and those of us who had experience in that line were appointed to take squads of men, drill them daily, and in a few days the regiment was organized with a quota of about 700 men.[16] Learning that the enemy were advancing in the Tennessee Valley, and had reached Courtland, our regiment then started on the march to Corinth, in good spirits and full of hope. We left LaGrange about April 20th. 1862,[17] and over hills and dales proceeded on the journey. The first evening the march was about ten miles– all night without tents. Next day all moved along at first rate speed as the weather was fine, and we soon reached Russelville Ala.[18]

There I met some of my relatives and it was a gladsome meeting. The stay there was of a very limited duration for the regiment started on the road again early next morning, moving on quite a distance, and at noon stopped to rest. I was fortunate enough to get under a good shade tree, and concluded to lie down on the pretty grass that was growing luxuriantly underneath its boughs. While in meditation, I felt something move beneath me, and also heard a hissing noise, then on looking around beheld a snake, which I suppose mistook me for a log, or something of the kind, that would be a suitable hiding place, but on discovering its presence, it is needless to say how quickly I jumped to my feet, and congratulated myself on having the good fortune to not be snake bitten. We still had a good ways to go, the weather became inclement, and then our fate was to be marching through rain and mud with soaked clothing. We reached Corinth after a real, disagreeable, and also round about journey of about a weeks duration.[19] Arriving at Corinth a camping place was selected and then we were in the midst of quite a large army, supposedly some to amount to about fifty thousand or more men. Regiment after regiment, brigade after brigade, and division after division, were encamped for miles around. Each morning and evening, numerous brass bands would cause the air to vibrate with their martial music, playing such tunes as Bonnie Blue Flag, Mocking Bird and Dixie, and then so often, the booming of cannon, with rattle of small arms could be heard in the direction of the enemy.

Arms were furnished, and our regiment (35th Ala.) was placed in Gen. Preston's brigade, with the 3d., 7th. and 8th. Kentucky regiments.[20] We found them to be as brave, and gallant set of men as men bore arms, and were glad to be with them. They called us yellow-hammers, and sometime afterwards they remarked that there was no need of being afraid to go into a fight with us, for they knew the yellow-hammers would stand their ground as long as any set of men. We had the same faith in them and was in no way disappointed in these opinions.

The Corinth country proved to be of a low, flat, craw-fish soil, at least the portion where we were encamped was of that nature, and the water was by no means good, which was so different from the pure running streams many of us had been accustomed to seeing, and drinking from in our own section of country, yet all managed to get along very well while encamped there.[21] We soldiers expected a big battle to commence almost any day, but that was not the program, so all on a sudden one morning[22] the Dixie army was in motion, having started down the Mobile and Ohio R.R. Our command got as far as Tupelo Miss., and then part of the men were ordered to go across to the Mississippi Central R.R. This was a tedious and tiresome journey, however, at last,

Oxford Miss was reached and there the troops were put on trains bound for Vicksburg Miss. . . .

[On the way to Vicksburg, Harmon witnessed the aftermath of a train derailment, "a sad sight . . . , for some seven or eight poor fellows had been crushed to death." At first Harmon thought the "little city" of Vicksburg to be "quite a nice place," but upon closer inspection it was "almost deserted," owing to the enemy's daily barrage of "heavy shells into the doomed place." His unit maneuvered constantly so as to escape the deadly blasts. One day a shell fell near his unit, unexploded, and some of his men decided to tamper with it, touching off an explosion, killing one and wounding several others. "I beheld the sad sight, and thought, how often do people have to pay dearly for folly, and thoughtlessness." Afterward, Harmon's regiment boarded a Southern Rail Road train for Jackson, Mississippi, and from there traveled south on the Mississippi Central to Louisiana, arriving at Tangipahoa on July 30, 1862, in time to participate in the assault on Baton Rouge. During the fighting Harmon not only had to contend with heavy enemy fire but also being stung by wasps. "The Good Lord spared me, I was not struck by any bullet, and I got rid of the wasps as soon as possible." At another point a man standing next to him was killed by a cannon ball, and "another passed so close by me that I was knocked over. . . . I fell on my hands rather stunned, but sprang up quickly as I could and went back to pick up my gun, and soon was with the men again. . . ." Following the battle, Harmon and his men moved on to Port Hudson, where they encamped, until being ordered to march back to Tangipahoa. This march was especially hard, "for rain fell nearly through the whole journey." Moreover, "many were barefooted, and as for myself my shoes gave out, and I had to walk over one hundred miles bar footed, with sores and blisters on my feet." After resting for a while, the regiment boarded a train for the return trip north to Jackson, where it remained for a week, before moving further north to Holly Springs, Mississippi, and finally Gray's Creek, a few miles from Grand Junction, Tennessee.]

6

Grand Junction, Tennessee

It was about a week's duration that we stayed at that location, and after resting were destined to make some trying and active movements. Gen. Van Dorn[23] was the commanding general at this time, and there must have been some four, or perhaps five thousand men assembled at that point awaiting orders. While camping at Gray's Creek a force of the enemy came to Grand Junction, supposed to be about three thousand men. Our commander[24] thought he would see if they would show fighting qualities; so all started off for LaGrange;[25] after reaching that place we were received joyfully by the citizens. The ladies seemed perfectly happy to see our flags waving around them. Great baskets of fruit were brought out and distributed among the men.

The enemy however had found out that our forces were approaching nearer than they liked, and perhaps fearing we might get in their rear, began to retreat. They were chased a considerable distance, but finding no fight with them, the chase was given up near a little hamlet north of Grand Junction[26] where all stopped for the night, greatly fatigued. A forced march of about thirty miles had now been made, and the nearest way to get back to camps was said to be twenty two miles. We laid out that night in an open field, with a heavy dew falling, on us, without blankets, feeling worn and sore.

Having passed the night in the best manner possible, the next morning a start was made for camps, which was reached during that evening.

There is little doubt but what the enemy would have been placed in a bad situation had we reached his rear, but he was too watchful to allow such as that to happen so all that was accomplished, amounted only to a few prisoners captured, several wagons and teams taken, besides giving them a good scare. Having reached camps our troops then rested about two or three days. It was now about the 26th or 27th of September, the fall was advancing and the weather was getting cool.

7

The Battle of Corinth

A junction with Gen. Price's forces had been planned with a view of making an attack on the enemy's forces at Corinth. Gen. Price[27] was there, somewhere in the neighborhood of Iuka Miss. Having prepared several days rations, and receiving marching orders, all then started in the direction of Ripley Miss. On Oct 1st 1862 camps were about six miles north of that place, and at this point Gen Price joined Van Dorn, with his forces. Our army then was within thirty miles of Corinth.

A report came at that time that the Federals had evacuated Corinth. Yet few believed it, but a strong belief existed that if they had not gone we would be able to make them go. The next day (Oct 2nd) all were on the advance, moving slowly and cautiously, for it was then found out that there was a strong force of the enemy not far off. Having arrived near a little station on the Memphis and Charleston R.R.; there the Federals were found to be in strong force, and prepared to give battle. Their lines were placed behind the rail road, which at that place served as excellent breast works. Lines being formed our men were ordered forward, and the battle commenced in earnest.

Our brigade charged a battery supported by a strong column of infantry, and then it was, we had desperate fighting. Their artillery fire was heavy, grape and canister was poured into our ranks besides a murderous fire from their infantry, made a field of death there, however our men began to yell and advance, every one loading and firing as rapidly as possible, and at last we got closely to them, for they had held their ground in a determined manner. The bold advance, and the deadly work that was going on, made them give away, and commence running with all the speed that was possible, and right there is where our guns made the greatest havoc.

Our men pursued them for a while and then stopped to rest. The losses in killed and wounded was heavy on both sides. Our company lost ten, and our regiment about forty.[28] The Captain of my company (Thad Felton) was killed,[29] he was a noble young man, and all regretted his loss very much. I was very near him when he was shot, the bullet struck him in such a fatal place, that he fell over and expired in a few moments; not even, seeming to know what hurt him. Our troops had routed them and captured their artillery but with severe loss. Our regiment was small, having been reduced by the incidents of war to about two hundred and seventy five in numbers. The enemy had been driven back into their entrenchments at Corinth, and a line was formed around the place. Night was drawing near, our portion of the lines was right among the enemy's tents, and what sleep the men got that night was in line of battle, with arms by their sides. The weather was cold, I was without a coat, therefore to keep from extreme suffering, I managed to cover with a portion of one of those tents, and it is almost useless to say that the night seemed a long and dreary one, for all had to stand it without fires, for it would have been very dangerous to have even had the smallest light.

Early in the morning cannonading commenced again, and the expectation was to go into another desperate fray. Daylight dawned, and the sun beamed forth in his glory. The booming of cannon and the rattle of musketry was going on at a heavy rate. All were keeping perfectly quiet at our position, but realized a bloody battle was going on at our left. It was desperate indeed, for there was a continued roar of musketry, and roaring of artillery, whilst our men were almost spectators to this awful scene, and expecting every moment a bloody task for us would come next. We were held as a reserve; the Generals did not see proper to put our division in this last day's fight.

There have been many battles where greater numbers were engaged, and where very hard battles have taken place, but I do not believe any field of slaughter can show forth more courageous fighting, and determination to overcome, than was shown on the gore stained field of Corinth. The Texas and Missouri troops were those engaged during the last day of this battle. These gallant men charged right up to the Federal strongholds, bristling with weapons of death, and hundreds of these brave men were shot down while attempting to scale the enemy's works, and the gallant Colonel Rogers of the 2nd Texas regiment followed by a few of his men planted the Bonnie Blue Flag right on top of a strong fort while he, and his men there met death. No wonder his enemies could admire such heroism, he was like Martial Ney, "the bravest of the brave."[30] This terrible slaughter decided the day, and we were forced to retreat, which fell to the lot of our division to cover.

The enemy had determined to harass our men as much as possible and to do whatever harm they could. They followed closely, and would make attacks on the rear guard every now and then. Their Cavalry, it seemed, were very desirous of trying to get our troops in disorder, so some of them had to skirmish with the Federal Soldiers every once and a while. As our forces proceeded on the retreat, there were two small rivers to be crossed, running in about five miles of each other, no doubt, they had hoped to produce confusion and thereby placing our army on a serious condition while trying to cross these rivers. Our commander being tired of such demonstrations as they were making decided to try and check them before reaching these rivers. So an ambush was set, the enemy came in considerable force; in an unsuspecting manner. Our skirmishers fought them so stubbornly that their skirmishers were driven back on the main line, and our skirmish line fell back of the men that were being in ambush, and would fire over these concealed soldiers, at the advancing enemy. All at once the ambush arose and gave the Federals several volleys, which sent them back in fast order. The shock was too great and caused a rapid retreat. They did not trouble us anymore, and all moved along unmolested towards Ripley, but had a very severe and tiresome time.

Our Provisions were exhausted, and many were hungry and foot sore, however on the journey the foragers had gathered some corn, in the ear, this was issued out among the men, which all were very glad to receive. When we stopped at night the only thing that could be done was to stick one of those ears of corn on a ram–, hold it over a fire, and cook the grains in this way. Corn was all that had been secured as provisions for several days, and some of it was eaten raw at times when we had no chance to have fires, nevertheless all were glad to even get raw corn. After several days hard marching our troops arrived at Holly Springs Miss, and went into camp near that place. There is one peculiar circumstance in regard to Corinth that made an impression on my mind. During the spring of 1862 my regiment was in camps there, and had to make a retreat, then after going the rounds through Mississippi and Louisiana for several months, we then returned to the same place, staid all night, resting on our arms, and next day had to retreat again after undergoing a terrible shelling from our enemies.

8

In Camp Near Holly Springs

Our troops reached Holly Springs about the 10th or 11th. of October, went into camps, where good tents were supplied, with straw to sleep on and thus they made out very well in that way, but had a bad time about getting water and wood, having to go about one half mile for water, and a considerable ways for wood. All staid there some three weeks or more, got a good rest, and felt in better spirits.[31] The following is an extract from one of my letters.

> Camp Cold Water
> Near Holly Springs Miss–
> Nov 1st 1862–
>
> My Dear Mother.
>
> As I have one more chance to send you a letter, I will embrace the pleasant opportunity and write to you, for I know you are anxious to hear from me. I am in good health and doing very well considering how every thing is during these uncertain and trying times. Our company has increased in numbers lately. We have now about sixty men, and our regiment has about three hundred, though there have been times on our marches that this battalion would be reduced to about one hundred and fifty. Gen Rusk is

now the Brigade Commander and we are in Lovell's Division.[32] The health of the regiment is very good, and the boys seem to be in good spirits. We are now ready to give our enemies another battle, when they so desire, yet it is to be hoped that fighting will ere long be no more, and that this cruel war will soon end. Let us sincerely hope that the leading men of both sides can come to an agreement, and that some compromise can be made which will result in an honorable peace, and this horrible sacrifice of human life may be at an end.

There has already been blood enough spilt, homes and firesides made desolate, and productive fields laid waste, with untold destruction of property to ruin the country for many years to come, yet if they will still persist in making war on us, and deny our rights, we will resist them to the last, and offer our lives on our countries' alter. Our people, I believe, are determined to pursue the right, to uphold it, and will not submit to unreasonable and unjust exactions, as it seems they would make on us. If we have to die let us die as freemen, and hold to principles which are sacred and just. Although we have been passing through a great many hardships, and have had some very trying ordeals, yet our men seem to be doing very well, and appear cheerful with a willingness to discharge whatever duties that are placed on them.

As for myself, I believe it can be said, without flattery, that I have been as good a soldier for the Confederacy as most any one, for the time I have been in the service. I have never been away from our regiment a single day, nor have I been excused from duty more than three or four times, and then not more than two or three days at a time. The regiment has never been on the battle field, or on a march, but what I have been with them. The Almighty has blessed me both with health and through dangers, yet how many of the strong, hearty, and robust looking members of our regiment have passed from this life into eternity both from sickness and the bullets of our enemies. Out of about thirty of the Cadets which enlisted in our company, only about seven are now left. In the Corinth fight alone, we had one killed and four wounded.

The troops remained near Holly Springs for some time, and enjoyed the rest very much; quarters were much more comfortable than formally, which of course gave all a chance to rest, and become in a better condition to undergo future hardships. News came suddenly, that a large force of the enemy were advancing down the Mississippi Central R.R., and from all accounts were quite a superior army to ours,[33] so the generals thought best to retreat rather than risk an engagement at that time.

9

March to Grenada

Our Army then began its march for Grenada Miss., followed closely by the Federal forces. They annoyed us nearly all the way, and the result was several close fights, however they were driven back each time without very much trouble. All arrived at Grenada and immediately began throwing up breast–, and the men soon felt that they were ready to meet them, in case they decided to make an attack, yet they did not come as was expected, for circumstances happened that was unexpected to them, which threw a blight over their operations. Gen Van Dorn made a very successful raid at Holly Springs, destroyed all their supplies at that point, besides capturing some fifteen hundred prisoners.[34] These reverses forced them to return to Memphis.

My regiment at this time was in Thompson's brigade, Rusk's division, and Lovels Corps. Our regiment in its rounds had been connected with three different brigades commanded as follows: 1st by Gen Preston, 2nd by Gen Buford,[35] and 3d by Gen Lovell. On account of the promotion of Gen Lovell, the command of our brigade fell temporarily on Col Thompson,[36] who was Colonel of a Kentucky regiment. Reinforcements were sent to this point to a considerable extent, and it was not long before some twenty five or thirty thousand men were assembled there.[37] On the 24th of this (December) month, our army was reviewed by President Davis.[38]

Accompanying him were Gen Jos. E. Johnston, Gen. Pemberton, and other distinguished officers with their staffs. The review was in an open field, and it was a grand sight to see such an army under inspection, it was also charming to hear the strains of martial music that were wafted on the gentle breezes from the various bands, whilst the many banners of the different regiments were floating gracefully in the air. It soon became evident to many that it would be our lot to stay at that point during the winter, however such did not prove to be the case, for all at last received orders to start for Vicksburg, and were landed in that vicinity

On Feb 10th, camps were struck at Edwards' Station fifteen miles from Vicksburg, which location was called Camp Rusk. The army at Grenada had been divided and the troops sent to different places. Gen Rusk, by this time had charge of our brigade. We were only at this point for a few days, and then orders were received to start for Louisiana....

[On February 23, 1863, Harmon and his men arrived at Osyka, Mississippi, one-half mile from the Louisiana line, before being ordered on to Clinton, Louisiana. Along the way the regiment had to contend with the elements, especially rain–"there was an abundance of water and mud through the whole of this long journey"– they had to wade waist-deep through several creeks, which "was no pleasant time." While marching through Clinton, Harmon's regiment encountered a number of "fine looking... ladies" who waved and cheered as the Rebs filed by, with one particularly "handsome girl" exhorting the soldiers: 'There are the ones to whip the Yankees. Kill a half dozen for me boys.' Harmon smiled, but upon reflection the words seemed to him a bit extreme coming from a Southern lady. "Her patriotic zeal had got a little higher than was necessary," he reminisces. Finally, on March 8, the regiment reached Port Hudson, 20 miles north of Baton Rouge, where it encamped for the remainder of the month. During this period Harmon grew sick and, "having chills, and ... [being] quite weak," he applied for a medical furlough. But he "gradually got well, and stuck to duty," undoubtedly

strengthened by a letter he received on March 28 from his parents in Florence, who sent him a flag and a bookmark for his Testament. A few days later, possibly on April 6, Harmon's regiment was on the move again, marching to the railroad which would transport them back up the Mississippi Central Rail Road to Jackson, Mississippi. Arriving at Jackson on April 14, the 35th was ordered to Tennessee, moving east by rail, steamboat, and foot to Montgomery, and eventually by rail to Chattanooga, Tennessee, where it joined Braxton Bragg's forces in their efforts to stop another Union onslaught led by Gen. William S. Rosecrans. Arriving in Chattanooga on April 18, 1863, Harmon ascended Lookout Mountain and marveled at the "commanding view" it provided of "quite a scope of country, enabling one to see for a long distance the surrounding territory." But a few days later Harmon's regiment received orders to come down to Chattanooga and to board a packed train back to Jackson and finally to Vicksburg, which was being besieged by Federal forces under Grant.[40] For several days the regiment remained on the march, constantly moving, having no idea "where they would be the next." During the night of May 15 Harmon and his comrades had to "sleep on their arms," and by the next afternoon until dark they were in the thick of the battle, not far from where General Tihlman was killed. By the end of the several days of fighting, Harmon was "completely broken down," without provisions, and "nearly starved." Soon, the regiment again wound up in Jackson, half of which had been destroyed and its environs made "a perfect waste." "Even the ponds of water had been ruined by the enemy," Harmon recalls, "for they would shoot down animals in the water and leave them there to pollute it." Harmon's men continued maneuvering, marching and countermarching, constantly on the move and skirmishing with the enemy. On June 11, 1863, they camped about eight miles from Canton near the Big Black River. On the 15th they were near Panther's Creek, where they remained until the surrender of Vicksburg the following month, when they again fell back to Jackson, helping to defend that town during a battle which lasted from July 14-17.]

10

Letter from Home

It was about July 17th all began to retreat from Jackson.[41] The enemy did not follow very far. Being unmolested we went along quietly and at last stopped at Morton Miss, there going into camps on July 26th., where the troops had a nice situation with good water. While here a letter came from home to me, with the good news, that all were well, this being always comforting to hear, and to know the dear home folks were blessed, and had enjoyed good health. One lady friend from whom I received a letter, among other things was speaking of her sweet–. In reply I said:

He may be all right, but a good many of those stay–– gentlemen often proved to be what some people call, 'No Good,' and of poor dependence, for men who hang around home, eat nice things, sleep on feather beds, wear kid gloves, and pretend to be such ladies' men, lack a good deal of being gallant and noble, and would not do to trust, for if a ball should whistle close to ones ears, he would sink down in a fit of fear. The best blood of our country are battling for our rights and enduring all the hardships it is possible for men to stand; these will be the ones for our Southern lassies to claim when this cruel war is over. If we gain our independence it will be through the hardest of fighting, and great bloodshed, and men who stick to duty will be, and ought to be, the honored ones of our nation.

After staying at Morton for a short while, all moved to Forrest Station, Miss. and on August 1st. went into camps there. It was at this place five months' pay was drawn which was due from the Government. Nothing transpired there of any importance. . . .

[Harmon's regiment next moved, possibly on August 17, to Newton Station, Mississippi, a "very poor country with nothing but piny woods and log huts," but it was "a nice location for camping" and, apparently, for religious services. "Many enjoyed from two to three sermons each day, and there were quite a number of conversions. . . . It was very seldom that we had such opportunities of a religious nature." Here they remained for about three weeks, until news of enemy troop movements caused Harmon's regiment to make a forced march in the rainy darkness to Canton, which they reached on or about October 5. With cold weather approaching, they decided to set up winter camp, erecting log huts with wooden chimneys daubed with mud. "Christmas was spent in these quarters, and often merry times were seen among the men."]

11

Thinking from Home

The new year of 1864 soon dawned and oh how each wondered what would be the results before it passed away. All were blind to those facts, and time alone would tell us, and God alone knew what it would be. On Jan 9th. I wrote to my mother the following letter:

My Dear Mother—

It is a great pleasure to have a chance of writing and sending a letter to you, and in meditating on home and the sweet associations there, monotonous camp moments vanish away for the time being. I have no special news to write, but must say I was exceedingly glad to hear from you, and have the pleasant assurance that all were blessed with good health, and that a kind and loving Providence had smiled on you through the trials, and dangers of these most uncertain times. We had a cold, wintry breeze last night, but were comfortably fixed near blazing hickory fires, and then my mind wandered back to Old Alabama, and Home Folks, thinking of the many happy hours spent there, in days past, and gone forever, and me thought it might be possible that you all were not so fortunate as myself, by having the comfort and advantage of such good fires, as I had learned the enemy have taken away so many of the horses and mules, which perhaps has made it difficult to get wood. I hope however such is not the case, trusting all are doing well, and comfortably situated. Our army down here ought to be very thankful, that they are allowed the privilege of being in winter quarters, while so many other poor soldiers are now taking the cold winter weather without shelter and fires.

[Here, Harmon reminisces about how he and his comrades entertained themselves during the long winter of '64, particularly how he and his two messmates began baking sweet potato and fruit pies and selling them at fifty cents a piece. They made between twenty– and thirty dollars in Confederate money a day, but hardly cleared that amount, as sugar sold for three dollars a pound and a pound of flour for as high as eighty cents. On January 26 Harmon received another letter from Florence, this time informing him that "the enemy had been committing some serious depredations amongst our people." "Such were the consequences of an inhuman war," he observes. Finally, after being quartered near Canton for nearly three months, orders came for Harmon's regiment to break camp.]

12

March to North Alabama

It was with a degree of sadness we left our winter homes,[42] however all started for the east, and marched day after day, during very bad weather, through rain and mud part of the time, and then sunshine the other portion. We had no shelter of any kind except the canopy of heaven, and enduring many hardships, as we plodded along this tiresome march. The old camp grounds at Morten, Forrest and Newton were passed, still pushing along on the journey towards Meridian, through a poor, and what might be called rather a barren country.

Mississippi then was about given up to the enemy, and they then began making raids into the interior, some of their cavalry coming as far as Meridian after our men has passed that place, and had taken camps near there. They stayed but a short time however, and fell back in the direction from whence they came. Now had an idea where the next destination would be, and all things seemed to be of an uncertain nature. After camping near Meridian for a few days, camps were broken, then the way was made for Alabama, and we were not long in reaching the Tombigby River, then arriving near the interesting little town of Demopolis.[43]

We found the people there of a very friendly and sociable nature, which caused us to be very much pleased with them. It was here that our regiment was put on detached service, being ordered to North Alabama for the purpose of breaking up some robber bands that were committing depredations, and infesting the mountain country, as well as that of the Tennessee Valley.[44] The balance of our troops were sent around to Georgia to reinforce Gen Jos E. Johnston who then was confronting Gen Sherman. We started out on our mission, realizing quite a rough time and at last reached the nice town of Tuscaloosa, on the Black Warrior river.[45] At Tuscaloosa a rest was taken for about three days. Some of us went around to view the place, and found it quite an interesting little city. Several different manufactories attracted our attention, especially one that was engaged in making hats for the Confederate army. Leaving Tuscaloosa we started north for the mountains, and the Tennessee Valley. It seems that this portion of the country had been deserted by both Federals and Rebels, only now and then some cavalry would appear first from one side, and then the other, but neither side would stay any length of time. So on this account the field was made a good place for robbers and thieves to flourish, for it was not often they had any soldiers to interfere with their depredations. The people were unprotected and many bold deeds of robbery were committed of the most atrocious characters.

Our mission was to see what could be done with such fellows that were infesting the country south of the Tennessee river. So onward the journey was pursued, going slowly over the mountains, and trying to find out all we could in regard to outlaws, and their habitations. It was not long before quite a number were captured that seemed to be of bad or very suspicious characters. These were put together and sent off under a squad of men. I never knew what became of them. It was a bad time to have to climb and descend so many steep, rough mountains and hills, and all were glad enough at night to take a rest whenever a camping place could be found.

After several days march all arrived at the edge of the Tennessee Valley. The weather was cold and had become inclement, but we pushed on and arrived near the town of Summerville. Snow began falling and soon the ground was well covered with a good coating of this icy material. Tents being unknown each one had to take it as nature gave it, and all through the long night it snowed on us. Being very tired many would scrape away the snow, then lie down on the ground and cook with blankets, while they would soon be covered by the fast falling flakes.

What sleep that could be had was realized only while the work of nature was bestowing a white envelope, in rather a bountiful way. The snow however was soon melting, then all were confronted with an abundance of mud, yet they pushed forward, trusting to have a safe arrival at Tuscumbia or its vicinity, for we were satisfied when the regiment reached that point, a good rest would be the portion. Having arrived there all right and selecting camps, a peaceful rest was realized, for there was no news of any of the enemies' troops being near, even on the other side of the river.

13

Capturing the White Horse Cavalry

After being there about two weeks, information came that a regiment of Federal Cavalry had arrived at Florence, just across the river. No uneasiness was given by this news, so all went smoothly on for a while. One of our Cavalry generals, who had charge of a brigade, (Gen Roddy)[46] would make his appearance in the Tennessee valley now and then, and was enabled to make havoc with any small detachments of the enemy. It being such a dangerous venture for them, was no doubt the cause of their not coming on the south side of the river. So it was only with robber bands that the people were troubled in that portion of the country.

Our regiment at that time did not number much over one hundred and fifty men for the numbers had been cut off distressingly short by various dangers and exposures, yet the few left, were tried and true to the cause. There was very little fear that any force of the enemy would make an attempt to attack us in the position selected, for all felt sure that the Federal troops on the north side of the river would not dare to cross over to make battle, although there were perhaps five or six to one of us. Our Colonel[47] got information at last that one company belonging to this Federal regiment, was on a foraging expedition some seven or eight miles down the river, learning where they would be camped on a certain night, he determined to cross the river and capture that company if possible.

Having selected about seventy five men, our little force started down the river for several miles to where there was an island in the river, and also where a flat boat could be obtained for crossing. About ten O'clock at night all were landed on the opposite shore, and soon were going through woods and fields in the direction of the enemy. After about an hour and a half of tramping, we came close to where they were camped, formed a line of battle and then advanced right on them quickly as possible. Their pickets, or rather sentinels fired, but we made a rapid rush and surrounded them, taking all by complete surprise, and capturing about fifty men with all their horses, guns, and other things.[48]

They seemed greatly mortified at their misfortune, but all they could do was to go along as prisoners. I learned one man was killed and also one or two wounded, having to hurry away so quickly and in the darkness, I could not tell exactly how this was, but hoped the wounded and dead would be able to have good care bestowed on them. We arrived safely again at the river bank where the flat boat was ready, and by day light all were landed over on the island. The horses had to swim across, but I believe they got across without having loss. At last all were safely landed on the south bank of the river, including prisoners, horses and other things captured. I had seized a fine young gray horse, which proved to be a noble animal, and it was quite a pleasure to ride him. The horses however were soon taken from us. Both prisoners and horses were sent to South Alabama, and this required a portion of the men to guard those captured while on their way to prison, therefore our numbers were still reduced, yet those that did not go south remained in camp a while longer.

14

A Visit to Florence

My home was at Florence, and I had not seen any relatives since I left them in the spring of 1862– a long time. It was natural that those who had homes across the river and were placed in a similar situation as myself should be very desirous to take the risk of going there to see their home friends. A report came that there were no Federals in Florence, and I, among others, made efforts to get leaves of absence to go across the river, and remain about a week. I obtained a furlough, made my way to the river, got a gentleman to carry me across in a small boat, and by a private way made for home. It was a joyful meeting, and proved one of the greatest pleasures of my life to meet the dear home folks again. . . .

My presence at home was kept a profound secret by friends there, for no one knew what time the enemy might appear in town, And sure enough after being at home for about two days a cavalry regiment came, and it looked as if they were going to stay for a while. Many of them went around to the different houses, and several came to our house, and I had to secrete myself in a garret, while they were searching the premises. They did not find me however, and as fortune would have it, left the town. I then began to conclude it was dangerous to remain much longer, but thought I would risk it two or three days more, everything seeming to be quiet in town. As no one could hear of Federals being around, I concluded to take a walk to Cypress Creek and go to a place called gunnel ford. A friend (Arthur Bliss,)[49] and once a schoolmate of mine, was my company.

We went through the woods, avoiding the road all the time, for fear we might meet some enemy. The ford was reached all right, and my friend went ahead to see if all was right, while I lingered backward in the bushes. He being a boy of some seventeen years of age, and a citizen it was not likely any one would disturb him, even if some of our enemies should meet him, however I was a Confederate soldier, and there was no telling what might be my fate in case of being captured, especially if it should be by some of the outlaws which were roaming through the country and going around under the guise of Union soldiers. As he emerged from the bushes, a company of guerillas in Federal uniform were in sight, right on the other side of the creek and ready to cross.

They did not see me, and I ran back into the woods, they therefore supposed he was alone, and began to question him some, asking him what he was doing there, he then told them he was just taking a walk. So after a few more words, they proceeded onward towards Florence, and then he came back to where I was in hiding. I then felt my position had been rather a dangerous one, for if they had captured me, men with such principles as those might have been guilty of shooting me on the spot. This company had the name of being a very dangerous band of robbers, so I thanked God for being spared, and not falling into their hands. I told Arthur that I must arrange to get back across the river to the regiment as quickly as possible; he then agreed to take me across in a skiff, that he knew could be obtained, and that was hidden under some bushes overhanging the river bank.

I went home and arranged to take my departure, so bidding home folks and other friends good bye, we went to the river, got possession of the skiff, and it was not long before he landed me safely across the other shore. I certainly appreciated his kind acts, and the interest he manifested in my behalf while at home. He was a noble and good boy, and long years have passed since I met him, but have learned that he made a most useful and valued citizen. Having made my way for my regiment, was soon informed they had started on their way for South Alabama, but it was not long before I caught up with them and joined in the long trip that was there before. We had been in the North Alabama country during a good portion of the spring of 1864. It was now the month of May, which seemed to be gliding swiftly away.

[On May 20, after a long march, Harmon's regiment stopped at Montevallo, Alabama , before moving on to Montgomery. Here they boarded trains to Dalton, Georgia, where they rejoined their division in the fight against Sherman's army during the Atlanta campaign. Presently serving in Scott's Brigade, Loring's Division, Army of the Mississippi, "It was now our lot when not on the march, to be in the ditches. It was continued flanking and changing positions. Skirmish after skirmish, with now and then hard battles going on, indeed contests in progress nearly all the time." Harmon recalls the scene from on top Kennesaw Mountain, from which one "could see vast columns of the Federal army for miles away." Held in reserve at New Hope Church, undoubtedly "the most severe engagement during the campaign," Harmon's division fell back to Marietta, where they remained under constant artillery bombardment until June 28, when Sherman's army "advanced in heavy columns of battle. . . in a determined and gallant manner," before being repulsed, leaving "quite a number of dead and wounded on the field." At Peach Tree Creek, on July 20, Harmon's brigade charged the Federals and lost a number of men, before they slinked back toward Atlanta and dug in. Finally, on September 3 the Confederates withdrew to Griffin, Georgia, conceding the "great prize" of Atlanta to the Federals. "What a horrible thing is war," Harmon observes.]

15

Hood's Tennessee Offensive

All was now quiet at Griffin, and both armies seemed to be taking a rest for a while, and as each one was wondering what and where would be the next blow, all at once we received orders to march, and then started out on the long and wearisome trip to Tennessee.[50] It was quite a surprise to us soldiers in realizing such a move was to be made, and no doubt the Federal Commander was surprised at the undertaking, yet it proved to be the very thing he would have desired. So he held his ground, while our forces were passing around him and going northward.

We continued the march, ever now and then striking the rail road and capturing a lot of their men that were found at different stations. No enemy followed, and at last all reached Northern Georgia, camping near Rome a while,[51] and then we made the way for North Alabama. It was certainly a long march over mountains hills and vales, a good deal of it being a barren country. At last our army reached the edge of the Tennessee River Valley, foot sore and very tired. Proceeding towards Decatur some of our men were soon near that town, where they found a detachment of the enemy. These were soon driven into the town,[52] and then the army moved onward towards Tuscumbia, and Florence, at last[53] reaching a point near Florence on south side of the river where all went into camps, remaining there some time and taking a good rest. A pontoon bridge was not long in being thrown across the river, and the whole army now got ready to cross over.[54] This was the largest bridge of that kind I ever beheld, and it was quite a sight to see an army of perhaps thirty five thousand men, crossing so large a river on a structure of this kind. Vast numbers of soldiers, batteries, and wagons were continually moving over it until all were across on the north bank of the river.[55] The troops went into camps at Florence for a while, and I then received a leave of absence to go and visit home folks again. It was another joyful meeting, and proved a most delightful time while there, but it then I met some of them for the last time, for Death claimed his own; we never saw each other again. How sad is life in many respects, and how changeable its course, for we never know what a day may bring forth.

The enemy had then left that portion of the country, and it was said that Columbia Tenn was the nearest point any could be found. They had been at Florence for some time before our arrival, but only a regiment or so would be about all that would come there. It was found out by some of our men that some of the negroes at Florence had been behaving quite badly and had become very unruly. One old negro by the name of Bob Leightford had been stirring up strife and inciting the negroes against the whites, so he was caught and taken to the woods and there hung to a limb of a tree. I felt sorry for this old negro, when seeing him hanging and dangling to that tree, which was a sight I never wished to see again, however it was claimed that the charges were very grave and there was every reason to believe they were true. After resting at Florence a few days the time drew near for our departure, then onward for Tennessee was the move to be made. It looked now as if some bold, some desperate military movements had to be executed, yes the strongest of efforts made to insure victory to our arms, and to brighten the hopes on which the cause rested.

Was it not possible (we thought) to invade Tennessee, capture the enemy's forces there and then have Kentucky and Tennessee in our possession? Such as this was hoped for, and many trusted that ere' long Confederate banners would be floating in the streets of Nashville. The army left Florence[56] with bright hopes for victory and success.

Cold weather was then setting in, however we bore it and marched on the way through inclement winds towards Columbia Tenn, and at last reached that vicinity, finding the enemy posted on the other side of the Duck River.

[Harmon's corps to which he belonged (Stewart's) encamped near Pulaski Pike, about two miles from Columbia, and it was here that Harmon obtained a 3- leave of absence so that he could visit some relatives living in town. Meanwhile, the Confederate army continued pushing toward Nashville. Separated from his unit, Harmon attached himself to the 3rd Tennessee Infantry Regiment, in which he served at Spring Hill on November 29. Arriving late at the battlefield at Franklin, Harmon is shocked by what he sees. "No one that did not see it could describe fully the horrors that was witnessed there, and the carnage that took place, in so short a time." It was here that he found his old regiment which had been "cut to pieces," "a great portion of them was lying dead and wounded. . . . Dead men were lying there in almost every conceivable position, and shot in almost every form imaginable, their wild and sad expressions, telling of the agonies they had endured."]

Our company suffered very severely, about one half being killed and wounded. Captain Stewart[57] was among the dead, he was a brave and true man and it was sad indeed to have to lose such a comrade. Another one of my company that was killed was Tommy Peebles[58] of Moorsville Ala, a most noble young man, and one whom we all loved. He and Capt Stewart were school mates of mine while attending Lagrange College. We had been together ever since the spring of 1862 and our associations had always been of the most pleasant and cordial nature. Through all hardships and trials we had tried to be true to our duties. Out of the twenty five of these college boys who enlisted in our company only three were then left. Some of the boys had with them faithful Negro servants who staid close to them, and when sickness and death came, their bodies were by such help taken back to their homes, which to say the least was a consolation to their friends and relatives, rather than to be buried in unknown graves. After burying the dead all prepared to leave Franklin as the enemy had made his course for Nashville, and soon the army was marching towards that city.

[Approaching within a few miles of Nashville, Harmon's brigade encamped behind a rock fence near the Granny White Pike and to the left of four field pieces of the Point Coupee, Louisiana, artillery, which was supported by the infantrymen. With food running out and with no winter clothing or shelter, the Confederates "stuck close to [their] colors," "determined to make the best of it as could be done under the circumstances." Harmon's unit was held in reserve on December 15, the first day of battle, but on the following day it suffered "the havoc and crash of . . . numerous missiles of death" from Federal batteries. "The cannon balls flew thick and fast, bursting all around, tearing ground, thus contending with those in front." Soon, Federal forces rushed the Confederate lines, capturing about two thousand men, including Harmon. "I can never forget the awful, yes horrible time we had to endure after being captured," Harmon recalls. Cold rain, open-air shelters, no fires, scant provisions were among the difficulties with which Harmon and his fellow prisoners had to contend, before they were placed in the Tennessee State Prison and later transferred to Camp Chase, Columbus, Ohio. "On this trip the men were badly crowded in box cars. Many were sick and quite a number died with pneumonia." At Camp Chase the men were placed in barracks, which were "as comfortable as any one could have expected," and there was a good supply of water and a place to bathe, but sickness– smallpox–, and there was never plenty to eat. "Retaliation for the way the Union prisoners were treated at Libby prison and at Andersonville, it was claimed as a reason why we were fed so poorly," Harmon explains. Meanwhile, the Confederate p.o.w.s got along the best they could, combating boredom and monotony by reading, making crude jewelry, attending religious services, playing cards, and "gambling with a game they called Keyno," until news reached them of Lee's surrender at Appomattox and the war ended. By

JAMES W. HARMON

mid-May, Harmon and his comrades, all "broken down and tired of an unholy war," were released from Camp Chase and boarded trains for the first leg of the long trip back home, or "at least the place that was called home."]

EPILOGUE

This ended my war experience of three years duration, and while about all Confederate soldiers went to destitute homes, not knowing how to do, or what could be done, still we could go home, or among friends or loved ones and make the best of the situation, and try by honest efforts and industry to make amends as much as possible for what had been lost, and trust to an all wise Providence, who does all things well to guide in that way which would result in the most good. The issues had been settled by the sword, never to be revived again.

Old Confederate soldiers went peacefully to their homes and firesides, there to follow their avocations of peace and love until the end should come. One by one they have passed away, and as autumn leaves many have fallen. A few more years will tell the tale, and none will be left. As a class, none at this present time could be found, that would be more loyal to their government, old issues are cast aside, and forgotten, and love of country predominates within their hearts. Their strong desires are that our land and country may be greatly blessed, that peace and prosperity may grow more and more, that our beloved land may become greater and greater in all that can make a people happy and contented, and that Christian principles may become so deeply implanted within the hearts of our People that much good may be done in the vineyard of our Master and great blessings be the result to mankind. . . .

NOTES

1. The questionnaires were transcribed and published in a five-volume set, but the transcribers omitted ancillary materials included with the questionnaires. See Colleen M. Elliott and Louise A. Moxley, trans. & eds., The Tennessee Civil War Veterans Questionnaires (Easley, S.C., 1985).

2. Biographical information concerning James W. Harmon has been gleaned from his questionnaire. He indicated that his father, Albert, had become disabled in 1853, when James was ten years old. Adjacent to Albert Harmon's name in a census taken on the eve of the war are the words "Idiotic– Excitement," a euphemism for mental illness. 1860 Census, Alabama, Lauderdale County, Florence, 30.

3. Official Register of the Officers and Cadets of the LaGrange Military Academy (Atlanta, 1861).

4. Richard H. Rivers, President, Florence Wesleyan University.

5. On April 27, 1861, at a public meeting in the Wesleyan Hall auditorium of Florence Wesleyan University, the Rev. William H. Mitchell, pastor of the First Presbyterian Church, delivered a speech to the "Lauderdale Volunteers." Leaving Florence on Sunday, April 28, the "Lauderdale Volunteers" arrived a week later in Lynchburg, Virginia, where they were mustered into Confederate service as Company H, 4th Alabama Infantry. William L. McDonald, Beginnings . . . of the University of North Alabama:

NOTES

The Story of Florence Wesleyan University (Birmingham, 1991), 34; Compiled Service Records (CSR), 4th Ala. Inf., Record Group (RG) 109, National Archives (NA).

6. Originally numbering 125 students and professors, "The University Grays," who wore gray uniforms with black cuffs and collars and black stripes down their trouser legs, drilled every day after classes, using W. J. Hardee's Rifle and Light Infantry Tactics as their textbook. In mid-May 1861 the company, now having been reduced to half its former size, was disbanded to allow its members to go home and to join other units. J. P. Cannon, Inside Rebeldom: The Daily Life of a Private in the Confederate Army (Washington, D.C., 1900), 2.

7. Alice Harmon (b. c1849) was one of James's three siblings. The others were Sarah (b. c1845) and Silas (b. c1847). 1860 Census, Alabama, Lauderdale County, Florence, 30.

8. J. Butler Houston (b. c1831), son of Dr. Pugh Houston, organized the "Lauderdale Rifles," which became on May 27, 1861, Co. D, 9th Alabama Infantry. CSR, 9th Ala. Inf., RG109, NA.

9. Edward A. O'Neal.

10. Robert McFarland (1836-1896) organized and commanded the "Lauderdale Volunteers" (Co. H, 4th Ala. Inf.) at First Manassas. A native of Londonderry, Ireland, and a graduate of Washington [and Lee] College, McFarland in 1858 moved to Florence, where he practiced law with James Irvine. Resigning his commission in April 1862, he later formed a cavalry company which served under Gen. John Hunt Morgan. Jill K. Garrett, A History of Lauderdale County, Alabama (n.p., 1964), 215.

11. Both 1st Lt. John Simpson, Jr. and Pvt. William S. Andrews had enlisted in Company H on April 28, 1861. Simpson (1829-1861)

was a son of a Florence merchant, while Andrews (c1842-1861), a son of Robert L. Andrews, was a student, presumably, at Florence Wesleyan University. CSR, 4th Ala. Inf., RG109, NA.

12. Pvt. James Jackson, Jr. (1822-1879), 4th Ala. Inf., was shot through the lungs at First Manassas. Later a lieutenant colonel and colonel of the 27th Ala. Inf., Jackson was captured at Fort Donelson, exchanged, and wounded during the Atlanta campaign (June 1864). After the war he served as a probate judge and as a state senator (1865-67). Pvt. Robert Watkins ("Wat") Foster (1837-1885), a medical student before the war, was the son of George W. Foster, owner of "Courtview." After being wounded in the foot at Manassas, he received a medical discharge in November 1861. Ensign Charles D. Stewart [or Steuart] (1832-1869?), who listed his occupation as "constable" at the time of his enlistment, also received a medical discharge in October 1861. Harry V. Barnard, Tattered Volunteers: The Twenty-Seventh Alabama Infantry Regiment, C.S.A.(Northport, Ala., 1965), 123; CSR, 4th Ala. Inf., RG 109, NA; Jill K. Garrett and Iris H. McClain, comps., Some Lauderdale County, Alabama, Cemetery Records (n.p., 1970), 138.

13. Joseph E. Johnston.

14. The 35th Alabama Infantry Regiment was organized at LaGrange, Alabama, on March 12, 1862. Stewart Sifakis, Compendium of the Confederate Armies: Alabama (New York, 1992), 103.

15. The 35th Alabama was mustered into Confederate service at Corinth on April 15, 1862. Ibid.

16. One of Harmon's comrades/classmates, Thomas W. Peebles wrote in his diary for March 24, 1862: "Drill, drill. It seems to be the word destined to appear oftenest in my journal and it is the

NOTES

word that comprises my day's employment." On March 26 he wrote: "Drilling is still our principal employment and it is likely to be for some weeks yet." The Huntsville Times, Sept. 11, 1955.

17. According to Peebles, Company B left LaGrange on April 14, 1862, at approximately 4 p.m. Ibid.

18. The company passed through Russellville around dinner time and camped at Cedar Creek on April 15. Ibid.

19. The 35th reached Corinth on April 23 and was armed with Belgium rifles and assigned to Preston's Brigade, Breckenridge's Division. Joseph N. Thompson Papers, Southern Historical Collection (SHC), Chapel Hill, N.C.

20. William Preston's Brigade, Breckinridge's Command, District of Mississippi, Department # 2 (June-July 1862).

21. Peebles wrote on July 15, 1862, from Vicksburg: "Not much fun did we have at Corinth, for the water was bad, the people were mean and frequently they marched us hard." The Huntsville Times, Sept. 11, 1955.

22. May 29, 1862. Thompson Papers, SHC.

23. Earl Van Dorn.

24. Col. James W. Robertson, former superintendent of LaGrange Military Academy, commanded the 35th Alabama until the morning of October 4, 1862. Ibid.

25. Lagrange, Tennessee, a short distance west of Grand Junction, along the Memphis & Charleston Railroad.

26. Bolivar, Tennessee.

27. Sterling Price.

28. For a list of casualties in the 35th Alabama at Corinth, see The Huntsville Confederate, Oct. 23, 1862.

29. From Franklin County, Thaddeus W. Felton, Jr., who graduated first in his class on July 4, 1861, had been one of ten cadets chosen by the superintendent of LaGrange Military Academy to help drill raw recruits who joined the 35th Alabama. Thompson Papers, SHC; Official Register of LaGrange Military Academy.

30. Marshal Ney of Napoleon's army.

31. The 35th remained camped at Holly Springs until November 30, 1862.

32. Albert Rust's Brigade, Mansfield Lovell's Division, Van Dorn-Price's Corps, Army of West Tennessee, Department of Mississippi and East Louisiana.

33. On November 2, 1862, Gen. U. S. Grant left Bolivar, Tennessee, advancing on Oxford and establishing bases at Grand Junction and Holly Springs, along the Tennessee & Ohio Rail Road.

34. Starting on December 20, 1862, Van Dorn's raid forced Grant's forces to withdraw, temporarily.

35. Abraham Buford.

36. A. P. Thompson.

37. By December 1862 Van Dorn had under his command at Grenada roughly 24,000 troops.

38. For a reference to the "grand and imposing review" of the army made by President Davis on December 24, 1862, see Lynda L.

NOTES

Crist, ed., The Papers of Jefferson Davis (Baton Rouge, 1995), 8: 560.

39. The division was ordered to Vicksburg on January 31, 1863. Thompson Papers, SHC.

40. This itinerary is questionable, inasmuch as Gen. W. W. Loring reported that the 35th Alabama was in Enterprise, Mississippi, on April 26, 1863. OR, Ser. 1, 24, Pt. I: 544.

41. On July 16, 1863, Confederate forces under Joseph E. Johnston withdrew from Jackson, Mississippi.

42. Possibly on February 4, 1864. See Barnard, Tattered Volunteers, 79.

43. Arriving at Demopolis on February 18, it was here, on March 3, that Governor Thomas H. Watts gave the Alabama troops a "rousing speech" intended "for encouragement only." Ibid., 24, 80; Cannon, Inside of Rebeldom, 114.

44. Both the 35th and the 27th Alabama were placed on detached service to North Alabama, for the purpose as Harmon stated and in order to recruit new troops into the army. Thompson Papers, SHC; Barnard, Tattered Volunteers, 23-24; Cannon, Inside of Rebeldom, 113.

45. Beginning on March 4, the 35th and 27th Alabama tramped approximately 20 miles each day, arriving in Tuscaloosa the morning of March 7. Barnard, Tattered Volunteers, 25, 80.

46. Philip D. Roddey.

47. Col. Samuel S. Ives (1836-1917) had served in Co. I, 9th Alabama Infantry before March 1862, when he enlisted in the 35th

Alabama and was elected captain of Company A. Advancing rapidly through the ranks, Ives assumed command of the regiment in 1863, when Edward Goodwin, a graduate of LaGrange College, who had succeeded James W. Robertson, died at Columbus, Mississippi. Originally from Center Star, Alabama, Ives was wounded five different times at Franklin, Tennessee, but was not captured.

48. This action against Co. G, 9th Ohio Cavalry, occurred near Florence on April 12, 1864. OR, Ser. 1, Vol. 32, Pt. 1, 662-63; Barnard, Tattered Volunteers, 26. Pugh Cannon described the total captured: "We got 42 men, 44 white horses, a lot of fine guns and pistols, and 30 and 40 horses and mules which they had taken from the citizens, besides quite a number of cattle."

49. Arthur Bliss (b. c1850) was a son of English-born Robert L. Bliss, a Florence druggist. 1860 Census, Alabama, Lauderdale County, Florence.

50. On September 29, 1864, Hood's army moved out toward Tennessee.

51. Hood's columns reached Rome on October 8, 1864.

52. The 35th Alabama suffered a total of four casualties killed and wounded at Decatur, in action which took place in late October 1864. Thompson Papers, SHC; Barnard, Tattered Volunteers, 84.

53. The 27th reached Tuscumbia on October 31, while all of Hood's army arrived by November 16, 1864. Thompson Papers, SHC; Barnard, Tattered Volunteers, 84.

54. The pontoon bridge was located about 200 yards above the railroad bridge, linking up with the island and from the island to the other bank.

NOTES

55. The crossing of the Tennessee River took place on November 20. Thompson Papers, SHC; Barnard, Tattered Volunteers, 84.

56. Early on the morning of November 21.

57. Sam Stewart from South Alabama fell "with four bullets in him." Thompson Papers, SHC.

58. Peebles, 3rd lieutenant, Co. B, 35th Ala. Inf., from Mooresville, Ala., was wounded on November 30, 1864, at the battle of Franklin and died on December 1. The Huntsville Times, Sept. 11, 1955.

www.ingramcontent.com/pod-product-compliance
Lightning Source LLC
Chambersburg PA
CBHW050045080526
44586CB00014B/1461